Life Lessons: The "I Am" Edition

Declarations for the Extremely Effective Entrepreneur

Written by Jah'Life Ali

Table of Contents

Dedicated to

my mother, Vanessa, who gave me life and taught
me many valuable lessons.

Introduction

Hello. My name is Jah'Life and I would love to share with you some of the many declarations I've made to myself over the years that I truly believe guided me to becoming a successful entrepreneur. These declarations were birthed from various lessons I'd learned from life. They say that life is the ultimate teacher; but I like to say that it is a wise person that learns from the lessons of others. Doing so can help you avoid pitfalls that others have succumbed to and get to success quicker by only taking the steps that led others to success.

The life of an entrepreneur is not always easy. It can feel like being stranded on a deserted island that only has one tree for shade...on the hottest day of the year...which also happens to be the longest day of the year...with only a bottle of hot sauce to drink. Now as you sit on the hot sand near the beach on this deserted island you notice a message-in-a-bottle wash up on shore. As you retrieve the bottle, and open it, you find that the note inside is addressed to you from the IRS stating that you owe 5 years of back taxes. THAT is what the life of an entrepreneur can feel like; but it doesn't have to. These declarations that I am sharing are the powerful words I speak out loud to myself which allow me to set my mind and the atmosphere in agreement with my desired outcome..which is success. Each and every day, I strive to be an extremely effective entrepreneur; and this is one of the things that assists in bringing that to past.

Consider making these same declarations to yourself and then follow the path before you that becomes clearer as you set your mind and the atmosphere in alignment with your purpose and your goals.

I Am

I Am Awesome

Speak greatness into your life. Be the "wow" factor. Wow reads the same way even when looking at it backwards.

I Am Beautiful

Be the image that you believe is desirable. When looking outside of self you've missed the mark, for real beauty is in the eye of the beholder. What are you looking at?

I Am Belief

To know a thing is far greater than to just think a thing. Believe it by being the thing and that is the same as knowing it.

I Am Complete

There is nothing more that you need. God has equipped you with all the tools you will need for this life.

I Am Desire

Go after the things you want by becoming the thing you're going after. Get into character and play the part.

I Am Determination

You are focused on the outcome and nothing can stand in your way. Stay focused on the results and that is exactly what will be.

I Am Energy

You are a source of movement. Nothing about you is still or stagnant. Address all concerns with forward movement and vitality. All your results reside in the actions you take. Be energy and stay moving.

I Am Equality

Want for others the same greatness, opportunity and wealth that you would want for yourself. The same eyes you look through when you admire someone else should show you the same within yourself. You are worth admiring too.

I Am Faith

Be the thing that you are believing in and know that it will come to pass because God says so.

I Am Fearless

Be fearless by using fear. Fear is false evidence appearing real. Let fear infuse your emotions by increasing your awareness. Be aware of your surroundings and the people in it. Use fear for its navigating of treacherous terrains and for its ability to lead you to the top as it guides you away from the bottom.

I Am Focus

When aiming for a goal, do not be derailed by other shiny objects. They are a distraction and will take you off course. Stay locked in on your target until you subdue it or until you decide that you should go a different route.

I Am God's Son

There was only one father who created the heavens and the earth. If there's another baby daddy...I'll pass.

I Am Happy

Happiness is a state of mind and a self-fulfilling prophecy. It can be added to by an outside source, but never created by an outside source. Aren't you glad God made you self-sufficient?

I Am Healthy

Healthy is more than physical, it is also a mindset. Think pure thoughts and ride the wave of positivity.

I Am Inspiration

Look within for your own excitement. Get excited about your life. Out of the millions of sperm cells that swam towards that egg, you were the one that bonded with it and manifested as a living breathing soul in this physical realm. The real joy and excitement is in you. Tap into your inner self and bring out what you have within. Mentally stimulate yourself to make things happen.

I Am Knowledge

You are a walking computer. Everything that you
see and that you are aware of has been created by
man. All information and blueprints have come
from the study of man himself. This is your
foundation now stand on it.

I Am Life

Your experiences make up your existence. Learn
to embrace all your experiences for doing so
ultimately leads to growth.

I Am Like God

Be fearless and all knowing. You are made in the
image and likeness of your Creator. You lack
nothing and have been given the world as your
canvas. Create that which you will, say it out
loud and call it into existence.

I Am Limitless

The only limitations are the ones you place on
yourself. You are created to have dominion and
control of all things...even your shortcomings.

I Am Living God's life

Life is to be lived god-like. Decide today to live
your life like your Creator. Be more giving and
understanding. Help those who are in need and be
great in all you do. Be a creator and create all
that you so desire. Live your best life. It's yours to
live.

I Am Made In The Image Of God

Your children are made in your image and your likeness. Question to oneself, "who might your father be that you too share his image and likeness?" If I had to choose it would be the Most High whom is He that does all things. in the beginning was the Word...that's my daddy!

I Am Love

Take action as love is more than just an emotion. Make your presence felt by others due to the joy you bring. People always remember how people make them feel, so make others always feel loved.

I Am Magnetic

Be attractive, even mesmerizing. Continue to work on your personal development because the more you develop, the more you attract.

I Am Mentally, Spiritually, Physically And Financially Free and Strong

The order of man starts with his or her spirit, and what's in their spirit shapes their mentality. This is the part of you where it starts and where it ends. The physical direction of your life will be decided upon by the way you externalize your spirit. Everything else will come to fruition by the result of your expression of your mental thoughts. Think Great and be greater.

I Am Noble

Live by your word. Be known for your actions and let those actions create a narrative that is worthy of praise. When you look in the mirror the reflection you see should show you that you are distinguished and that you are honorable. Always leave your home in the morning with the posture of nobility.

I Am Peace

Be the absence of confusion. Drama is meant for the stage, not your natural or spiritual life. Keep the parking lot of your mind clear of the toxic car with the leaky transmission and oil spillage. Opportunity can't find a space in a parking lot filled with problems and excuses. Be the calm to the storm. It's exceptionally more inviting.

I Am Power

Be more than muscles. Be the source that gives strength to others. Be a person of influence to the point that people around you applaud and seek strength from you which will ultimately add to you tenfold.

I Am Qualified

Your experiences in life either qualify you or disqualify you. What are your qualifications? This will be measured by your accomplishments not necessarily the school you went to or the piece of paper you obtained. If you do something enough times you will end up qualifying yourself.

I Am Royalty

Do right by others. Be courteous and rule with empathy. Be a great thinker and listener. Be courageous and humble. The people will select you and call you their leader.

I Am Supreme

Seeing yourself on top is not the same as looking down on others. Don't confuse the two.

I Am Thunder

There is a place and time for silence. However, there is a time for the world to emphatically know you exist. Be loud and be heard. For the world shall know your name.

I Am Thoughtful

The thought is the beginning of all things. What you think about, you bring about. Take a moment and do an inventory of your surroundings. Surprise! Your current position in life is the sum of what you think most about. Change your thoughts and change your position.

I Am Victorious

The victory is yours. We all have been a victim of some kind, but in order to be victorious one had to be challenged by an obstacle. Remember that God said the victory is yours.

I Am Unconditional Love

Your emotions also lead to your actions. They are an expression of how you feel about a person, place or thing. Oftentimes, surrounding circumstances can change or impact those emotions. However, when adding the idea of "unconditional" there are no determining circumstances. It's love with no conditions. It is pure love.

I Am Water

Water is one of these most powerful of the natural elements. Whether you are still water or flowing water you impact and shape all that is around you. Be clear and transparent. Be focused and consistent. Nourish life and change the face of the world with your power.

I Am Wealthy

Money isn't everything but you should definitely have your share.

I Am Wisdom

To know and have the information is one thing. However, the application of information and knowledge is wisdom. Wisdom is more than wise words being spoken but more so acting upon the knowledge gained.

I Am Worthy

God created you to be priceless. To see yourself less than you were created to be is self-sabotaging. Know your value. It pays off.

I Am A

I Am An Asset

Become a person of value so that your very presence alone will produce residual benefits.

I Am A Boss

The decision is yours to make because you are the one that is in charge; but there is wisdom in listening carefully to those around you that can offer wise counsel. This will help you make the best decisions.

I Am A Cipher

Everything that goes around comes around. Acknowledge and respect this declaration for it all ends up back with you. Your wins and your losses. You are complete within yourself.

I Am A Creator

The sooner you know this, the quicker you will be able to self-direct the outcome of your existence and the things in it. Wherever you are at in life, remember that you created it.

I Am A Doer

Get up, get out, and do something. A closed mouth does not get fed, but an open mouth will get caught by what is chasing you down.

I Am An Example

I remind myself daily that someone is watching me.

Live your life in such a way that others will desire to follow. They say, "monkey see, monkey do". There is nothing wrong with being a copycat, just be sure to copy the right cat.

I Am A Go-Getter

When you see something of great value, go after it. Laziness doesn't live here. If it is within your scope of vision, then it's attainable. The target has been established. Now go hit it!

I Am a Great Husband (Spouse)

Keep your wife(spouse) covered. Protect them with your own life. A good spouse is worth more than 10 times the amount of money sitting in the Reserve Bank. A good spouse is irreplaceable. Don't let them out of your sight once you have one. They will be your master key to unlock many doors.

I Am A Jewel

There is a nugget in each and every one of us. However, sometimes its deeper than expected. Therefore in order to reveal this undiscovered nugget one has to go through some refinement. The refinement process can include lots of pressure and extreme heat. Disruption almost always follows intention. So remember, before your goals and dreams materialize, there may be some obstacles and challenges.

I Am A Leader

Become a great follower and in time you will be leading those you followed. Be an admirable example to those who are under your command; and always remember that the leader is the first person to take action.

I Am A Listener

Your ears are the gates to your soul. Guard your soul by policing what you allow to enter through your ear gates. Take in only that which you look to produce. Greatness put in equals greatness brought out.

I Am A Protector

There is a time for war and there is a time for peace. It's important that you know the difference. Attack with fervor when life is threatened.

I Am A Provider

A farmer tills the earth to feed not just himself, but those that are around him.

I Am A Rainmaker

Anyone can throw money in the air, but can you make it rain...literally? Be the person that nourishes those around you, where anything and everything around you grows. All the grass is greener everywhere because of you.

I Am A Speaker

Speak not for the sake of just making a sound. Have something of substance to say. Know that when you speak it is for the necessary communication of information. Your words should lead to creation. Don't underestimate the power of the tongue. It is the means by which things come into existence. Be cautious of the words you speak. They will visit you one day.

I Am A Survivor

Life consists of challenges and obstacles. They are geared toward the living only. As long as you are alive you will experience them. So best you embrace the challenges and accept them. The day that they cease to exist so will you. To survive is to thrive.

I Am A Teacher

Be a reflection of what you desire to see in others. Someone is watching you and picking up what you are demonstrating. Stay mindful and be the demonstration.

I Am A Winner

No matter the rankings, wherever you stand, you are first. No trophy nor selection defines you.

That determination was made before you were even born. You are here. You already won.

I Am A Writer

An accumulation of words written is more than a description of a matter but the conception of that which is being described. Take not lightly the power of the writer for it is the writer who gives birth to his or her words. Write it down and make it plain. The universe will do the rest.

<u>I Am The</u>

I Am The All In All

All that exists within you and about you exist in your Creator as well as all that exists in your Creator exists in you. You're not just a winner. You are everything that makes up a winner and beyond.

I Am The Answer

Every question has an answer and you're it. Be sure to dig within when looking for confirmation. God placed in all mankind his own treasure. Discover that answer and live life like it was meant to be lived.

I Am The Bag

Money has been the objective since its conception. However, those who accumulate lots of it have done so by becoming more and adding value as well as seeking after and achieving their dreams and goals. When their dreams and goals produce something that others find of value, then the market will happily exchange their dollars for it.

I Am The Best Father

A father does more than get his wife pregnant. He nurtures the seed and the mother the way he was designed and meant to. He tends to their needs in humility and by his strength. He is the foundation and leads by example.

I Am The Cause

Look closely in the mirror. It's you who gives rise to action. Everything starts and ends with you. You are the one that sets all things in motion.

I Am The Challenge

You are the iron that sharpens the steel. You provide the roughness that smooths things out. To chop down a tree, you must first sharpen the axe. Spend more time sharpening the axe in order to spend less time cutting down the tree.

I Am The Chosen One

Those who are chosen have chosen themselves first. Choose to be happy. Choose to be loved. Choose to be healthy and to be wealthy. You can possess all these attributes and more...the choice is yours. Choose yourself.

I Am The Director

You give the guidance while others act upon them. Everything around you is yours to direct and place where it should go. If something or someone is around you that you don't like, remember you are the one that placed it or them there.

I Am The Dream

Create the life that comes to you while you are asleep. Revelation comes to you at rest so be still often, because there is less distraction for your third eye. Your third eye is your mind which is the womb of your creation. Plant the seeds during the day in your conscious mind and let your subconscious give you the image that you are to manifest.

I Am The Editor

The "written by" credits belong to you. You have the authority to write people into your script and to write them out of your script. Nothing is in stone until you say so. There will be many characters applying for rolls. Choose the people that can act out your script. Choose wisely. You want your life to be spectacular, not a spectacle.

I Am The Effect

Wherever you are in life know that you were the director of the script. The great thing is you have the ability to cast a new role if you're looking for a new part.

I Am The Fire

Be the heat that creates the smoke and the flames. You have control of both. Smoke will let you know something is coming while the fire will let you know something is here. Fire can be used for your advantage because it will purify and refine. But also know that fire can also destroy. With that being said, kids shouldn't be allowed to play with fire.

I Am The Fountain

Provide refreshing thoughts by renewing your mind daily. Allow your thoughts to be the stream that others can come to and quinch their thirst.

I Am The Garden

Make sure your soil is fertile so that you will have a good harvest. Be attentive to the seeds planted so that the fruit you grow will be nourishing to yourself and others.

I Am The Gift

Be a giver and give yourself away. Be approachable and pleasant at all times. People should feel special by your presence alone. It's not every day that they meet someone as awesome as you.

I Am The Glory

Your existence is the evidence that there is a God. Proclaim His glory and be lifted in it.

I Am The Key

Be the key that opens more than doors and locks but be the master key that unlocks the fortune inside of you. You are the key to life, the key to love, the key to living, and the key to no limits. Use the master key that God gave you... it works

I Am The Lesson

Learn from your past encounters. What you've been through makes for a good case study.

I Am The Light

Because of you, people will be able to see their hands in front of their face. Be a brilliant person that illuminates the dark places around you so others see where they should be going and not stumble.

I Am The Master Key

Anything worth having should be locked and secured. Yet, there is an instrument called a master key that unlocks all doors. You are the master key that has the ability to gain access to all that is to be desired. Nothing is out of your reach.

I Am The Movement

Always be in motion. Being still and sedentary leads to atrophy and atrophy brings about loss and death. Constant motion creates momentum, which causes speed in the direction you desire to go.

I Am The Network

Cast out your net so others can join you. Build relationships with those you come in contact with and watch how your network grows your net worth. Alle means work to an end.

I Am The Obvious

Duh!

I Am The One

Everything starts and ends with you. You are the foundation to everything in existence. As it is above, so it is below. You carry the weight of all that is around you, so make your load lite.

I Am The Originator

There may be others that look like you, but no one else is you. You are the only copy of an incredible creation. The origin starts and ends with you. With that being said, start with the end in mind and work backwards to get to the beginning. You just created your roadmap. Now begin putting the pieces back together in reverse order and you will find yourself living in the results that you created originally.

I Am The Prize

You are valuable and everyone will seek after you. Some people will pay money to see and hear you. They will fight to be near you because they see that proximity to you is an achievement.

I Am The Producer

You determine the outcome of your life by the value you create in it. Create your life the way you would a movie. Make it worth seeing and people will exchange their dollars to view it.

I Am The Proof

All things are possible. You woke up today...there is your proof.

I Am The Question

Become your why. Whatever that why is, become it. Your why should fuel your drive when the tank is empty. Fill up with your why and let it carry you to your destination.

I Am The Rain

Water is more than a substance that makes things wet. It cleanses, nourishes, and can even shape certain elements. Rain is a consistent dripping of water and it is this consistency that allows rain to penetrate some things. Be rainwater and be a vital part of the ecosystem which comprises your community.

I Am The Rock

Be firm, yet gentle. Be tough, yet smooth. Be cool, yet warm. You are the foundation so stand your ground.

I Am The Solution

When all else fails outside of you, resort back to the real change factor which is you.

I Am The Source

No need to look further than your nose because you are it. You are the person from which good things come. You are fueled. You have an unlimited supply given by God himself.

I Am The Story

There is history, the mystery and then there is
your story. The greatest story that will ever be
told is the one you tell. There is only one you.
Yes, there are stories that are similar to yours but
none that are exactly the same. Know that each
story has its own amount of influence. Your story
needs to be heard because it contains help for
someone else.

I Am The Sun

Be the light of all lights. Your light gives light to
others. Your light will distinguish you from others.
Be the outlet, not the plug.

I Am The Test

You are the greatest study. Look within and you
shall find the cheat sheet.

I Am The Truth

It has been proven that you are already a winner
by your very existence alone. Your existence
needs no explaining it is real. Nothing about you is
false evidence appearing as real. Your presence is
the truth.

I Am The Voice

What station are you on? Tune into the channel
with the highest frequency and listen to its
direction. Be sure that you're being led by the
right voice.

I Am The Way

Everything must come through you before it materializes. You are the guard of your own port. If it landed on your dock, you allowed it to be there.

I Am The Wind

Everything you do shouldn't be seen or doesn't have to be seen. Be the invisible force that is drawn up by the movement of all things around you. Use it for good.

I Am The Word

Become one with your word. If you say you will do something, do it. If you say you will be something, be it. In the beginning was the Word and words sound power. When you send your words out into the atmosphere, they connect to the matter that exists in a prescribed way to make what you declared come to pass. Controlling your words is like controlling your destiny. Words have a funny way of manifesting after their own kind.

I Am That

I Am That I Am

Whoever you say that you are, you are and it shall be. Remember this the next time you go to say something self-deprecating. A foolish person self-sabotages. Only speak positive words over yourself and others. Speak words that will appreciate your value, not depreciate it. Choose pronouns that best describe you at all times.

I Am "Poetry"

WHO AM I

Who am I you wonder
I am the master, I am the writer
The more I write I evolve higher

Who am I you wonder
I am the man in woman, the under in stand
I am the master plan
I am the masterpiece and master mind
Looking at my watch, I am the creator of time

Who am I you wonder
I am the offspring of the Creator
I am the great of the Greater
I am His descendent
I am the act of my repentance
I am as Moses parting the sea with his rod
I am the evidence that there is a God

Who am I you wonder
I am made in the image and likeness of Him
I am living the rest of my life above the rim
I am the leading role
I am fearless amongst the bold

Who am I you wonder
I am the determining factor
I am the one that really matters
I am the power within
I am the beginning to an end

Who am I you wonder
I am the map of the way
I am the words I say
I am the missing link
I am that which I think

Who am I you wonder
I am the memory to remember
I am the root to the tree so no TIMBERRRRRRR!
I am the top to the bottom
From the bottom to the top
No more standing on the block
Now I buy the block

Who am I you wonder
I am the editor-in-chief
I am the faith with belief
I am the winner in win
I am the best friend

Who am I you wonder
I am the yellow in black
I am the truth in fact
I am the manual to this script
I am the one who wrote this shi*!

Who am I you wonder
I Am...is your answer!

DEAR MAMA, I AM

Dear mama, I am
I am the image and likeness of you
Yes, I am living out my dreams
I am the one though it seems

Dear mama, I am
I am your son the sun that shines
I am in front no longer behind
Yes, mama, I am the one indeed
Knowledge of self is what I feed

Dear mama, I am
I am my brother's keeper
Together we are an incredible force
We strengthen each other daily
All while keeping God as our source

Dear mama, I am
I am the voice of inspiration
That brings life to those in need
I am the solution for every problem
And water for the planted seed

Dear mama, I am
I am the father of wonderful children
And the protector of a beautiful woman
I am the example for those I lead
Man, I am really something

Dear mama, I am
I am at the top of the mountain
Having the most beautiful view
I am raising future leaders
I am standing here with you

Dear mama, I am
I am training students to be strong
To never give up or quit
Finding the muscle within
And challenging oneself to keep the fire lit

Dear mama, I am
I am using my influence
To build my business connects
And as long as I move consistently
Success is what I can expect

Dear mama, I am
I am sharing the mic with great women and men
Present in the moment
Together we're a part of a movement
And all those around us even know it

Dear mama...I am.

I Am...

Now its time for you to personalize this journey. What other declarations can you make over yourself to empower you towards success?

I Am...

____

____

____

____

____

I Am...

____

____

____

____

____

I Am...

____

____

____

____

____

I Am...

____

____

____

____

I Am...

____

____

____

____

I Am...

____

____

____

____

I Am...

____

____

____

____

I Am...

____

____

____

____

I Am...

____

____

____

____

____

I Am...

____

____

____

____

____

I Am...

____

____

____

____

____

I Am...

____

____

____

____

I Am...

____

____

____

____

I Am...

____

____

____

____

I Am...

____

____

____

____